# *Claire's* CONFECTIONERY

## CLAIRE ATTRIDGE

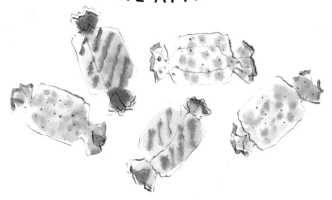

Macdonald Orbis

*For Elizabeth, who ate the sweets*

A Macdonald Orbis Book

First published in Great Britain in 1987
by Macdonald & Co (Publishers) Ltd
London & Sydney

A member of BPCC plc

Conceived, designed and produced by
The Albion Press Ltd

P.O. Box 52, Princes Risborough, Aylesbury, Bucks., HP17 9PR

*Editor: Jo Christian*      *Consultant: Jan Buck*      *Designer: Linda Sullivan*

© The Albion Press Ltd 1987  © Illustrations: Claire Attridge 1987

British Library Cataloguing in Publication Data
Attridge, Claire
Claire's confectionery.——(Claire's kitchen).
1. Candy    I. Title    II. Series    641.8'53    TX791
ISBN 0–356–14875–0

Typeset by Wyvern Typesetting Ltd, Bristol
Colour origination by Culver Graphics Litho Ltd
Printed and bound in Italy by New Interlitho

Macdonald & Co (Publishers) Ltd

Greater London House  Hampstead Road  London NW1 7QX

# · CONTENTS ·

Sweets are among the most appealing items to make at home yourself — not only are they delicious to eat, but they look attractive; and people who don't have time to make such luxuries for themselves greatly appreciate them as gifts. You won't believe how much better home-made sweets can taste than the shop-bought kinds until you've tried them for yourself!

The recipes given here fall mainly into the two major categories of confectionery making: managing melted chocolate, and dealing with sugar syrups. Neither is especially difficult, but there are certain rules about how these materials behave when they are heated and cooled which you will need to know if your sweet-making is to be successful.

**Melting chocolate**  The most important thing to remember when you are melting chocolate is to be careful not to burn it. Don't try to melt it too fast. Place it, in pieces, in a bowl set over a pan of hot water, off the heat. After 15 minutes or so, it should have melted sufficiently for you to stir it smooth and use it. When you are dipping sweets, nuts or fruits in chocolate, leave the bowl over the hot water so that it stays melted — you may need to replenish the hot water from time to time if the chocolate begins to set.

Several different types of chocolate are available, and they may at first be confusing. Professional confectioners use a very hard, top-quality chocolate called *couverture* for dipping, and this certainly gives the best taste and appearance to chocolates. However, handling *couverture* is a special skill which has to be learned.

Dark, light and white chocolate-flavoured bars and buttons which are specially made for dipping and moulding are available from trade suppliers and specialist kitchen shops, and they make a good second choice. They are easy to use, melting to the right fluid consistency for dipping, they set to make a thin, glossy coat and they have a good flavour. You can also use high-quality eating chocolate. It does not melt to such a thin consistency, so it is more difficult to use for dipping, and the finished chocolates will not be so glossy, but otherwise they will look attractive, and they will taste fine.

**Sugar syrups** A great many sweets are made from sugar syrups, with added ingredients which help to determine the texture and the flavour. The syrup is made by boiling sugar and water so that the water evaporates — other ingredients are either put in the pan at the same time, or added later. As the water evaporates and the sugar concentration increases, the boiling point rises. So the temperature to which a syrup has boiled indicates its moisture content, and how hard it will be when set. Syrup boiled to a low temperature makes soft sweets such as fudge (page 26), while high-temperature syrup sets to a hard consistency like that of barley sugar (page 33).

Getting the temperature right is, therefore, critical. A sugar thermometer, marked with the different recognized stages that the syrup goes through, is a great help (always warm it in hot water before putting it into hot syrup, or it may crack). But it is a good idea also to test the consistency, since the addition of any other ingredients to the basic sugar and water can change the temperature at which a particular stage is reached. Before you test a syrup's consistency, remove the pan from the heat and dip its base into cold water to arrest cooking. It is best to do this slightly before the target temperature has been reached, just to be on the safe side and prevent overcooking. If the syrup has not reached the right stage, return the pan to the heat and test again when the temperature is slightly higher.

**Soft ball**   112°–116°C/234°–240°F
Drop a teaspoon of syrup into a bowl of iced water. You should be able to shape it into a ball under the water, but it will immediately lose shape when taken out.

**Firm ball**   118°–121°C/244°–250°F
Drop a teaspoon of syrup into iced water and shape it into a ball. When taken out of the water it should feel fairly firm, and keep its shape for a few seconds. It will feel sticky.

**Hard ball**   121°–130°C/250°–266°F
Drop a teaspoon of syrup into iced water and shape it into a ball. It should be shaped easily and hold its shape at room temperature. It will still feel sticky.

**Soft crack**   132°–143°C/270°–290°F
Drop a teaspoon of syrup into iced water, then remove it. Stretch it between your fingers. It should separate into hard but stretchy strands, and feel only a little sticky.

**Hard crack**   149°–154°C/300°–310°F
Drop a teaspoon of syrup into iced water, then remove it. It should be a solid piece that will snap crisply when you bend it. It will not feel sticky.

**Light caramel**   160°–170°C/320°–338°F
Pour a spoonful of the syrup from the pan on to a white plate. It should be the colour of clear honey.

As you boil the sugar and water, it is essential to brush down the sides of the pan occasionally with a pastry brush that has been dipped in cold water. This stops stray splashes of syrup from drying on the sides of the pan; if they do, the syrup may form again into crystals of solid sugar, a process called crystallization. If these then fall into the syrup they could cause the whole batch to crystallize.

It can also happen that a syrup crystallizes as it cools. You don't need to worry about this when you are making soft, grainy sweets such as fudge — indeed, fudge is beaten after it has cooked to encourage crystallization. But if you are making sweets with a smooth texture you may need to add what is called an 'interfering agent' to the syrup to help prevent crystallization. Liquid or powdered glucose (obtainable from chemists) is the most reliable interfering agent. Other ingredients which interfere with crystallization are honey; milk, cream and butter; lemon juice and cream of tartar.

**Special equipment**   For melting chocolate, no special equipment is necessary. A specially designed dipping fork (available from kitchen shops) makes dipping and decorating chocolates easier, but you can use an ordinary table fork.

For boiling sugar syrups you will need a good pan which is big enough to allow the syrup to boil without spilling over and which has a heavy base to distribute heat evenly and prevent the syrup from sticking or burning. Very experienced cooks may be able to do without a sugar thermometer, but they don't cost much and they make it easier for you to know when your syrup is at the right stage.

A square or oblong tin is convenient for sweet-making: 15–18cm/6–7inches square is a generally useful size. But though many of the recipes specify this size for the quantities given, this is a general guideline, not a rigid instruction.

**Presentation**   The appeal of confectionery lies almost as much in its appearance as in its taste. So take a bit of extra trouble and present your sweets beautifully. Choose pretty plates or dishes to display them. If they need wrapping, use cellophane to show off lollipops or sticks of barley sugar, and attractive crinkled paper cases for dipped chocolates or truffles. Packed in beautiful glass jars and stoppered, a selection of your home-made sweets would make an unusual and delicious present. And you don't *have* to wait for the spring to make Easter eggs!

**Further reading**   Keen sweet-makers will find more information about confectionery, and many interesting recipes, in *Confectionery* (The Good Cook Series, Time-Life Books, 1981) and Shona Crawford-Poole, *The Sweets Book* (Collins, 1986).

# · COCONUT ICE ·

*450g/1lb granulated sugar*
*150ml/¼pint milk*
*150g/5oz desiccated coconut*
*a few drops of cochineal*          Makes about 700g/1½lb

Butter or oil a 15–18cm/6–7inch square tin. Cook the sugar and
milk together over a moderate heat, stirring often, till the sugar
has dissolved, then boil the syrup to 116°C/240°F, the soft ball
stage (see page 10). Take the pan from the heat, quickly stir in
the coconut and pour half the mixture into the tin. Stir the
cochineal into the rest of the mixture and pour the pink
coconut ice on top of the white layer. Mark the coconut ice
into squares or oblongs when it has cooled a little. Cut it up
when it is quite cold. Keep the sweets in an airtight container.

*juice of 2 lemons (about*
*    150ml/¼pint)*
*juice of 225g/8oz raspberries*
*    (about 150ml/¼pint)*
*50g/2oz powdered gelatine*

*125ml/4fl oz cold water*
*175g/6oz granulated sugar*
*6 tablespoons liquid glucose*
*caster sugar to coat (optional)*
Makes about 450g/1lb

Squeeze the juice from the lemons and strain it through a
nylon sieve. Put the raspberries in a heavy saucepan, cover it
and heat the fruit very gently for about 10 minutes, till the
juice runs. Strain the juice. Sprinkle the gelatine on to the cold
water and leave it to soften for 10 minutes.

Put half the sugar and half the liquid glucose in a saucepan
with all the lemon juice. Set the pan over a low heat and cook,
stirring frequently and occasionally wiping down sugar crystals
from the sides of the pan with a wet pastry brush, till all the
sugar has dissolved. With the pan still over the heat, gradually
stir in half the softened gelatine. Stir till the gelatine has
melted. Sprinkle a shallow 15–18cm/6–7inch square tin with
cold water and pour the liquid jelly into it. Leave the jelly in
the fridge or in a cool place for a couple of hours to set.

When the lemon jelly has set, put the raspberry juice in a pan
with the rest of the sugar and liquid glucose. Cook over a low
heat, stirring and brushing down the sides of the pan as before,
till the sugar has dissolved. Stir in the rest of the gelatine and
continue to stir until it has melted. Take the pan off the heat,
leave the liquid for a minute or two to cool slightly, then pour
it evenly over the lemon jelly. Leave the two-layered jelly for
several hours, or overnight, to set firmly.

Loosen the jelly by running the point of a knife round the
edges of the tin. Turn the jelly out on a cool work surface and
use a sharp knife to cut it into squares. If you like, finish the
jellies by rolling them in caster sugar. Plain jellies begin to get

rather tough after about a day, so eat them while they are fresh. Sugar-coated jellies will stay in good condition, in a cool place, for a few days.

The juices of other berries, such as strawberries and blackcurrants, and of citrus fruits, such as oranges and limes, also make delicious jellies, either single-flavoured or layered.

1 egg white
225g/8oz granulated sugar
75ml/3fl oz water
175g/6oz ground almonds
1 tablespoon lemon juice
2 tablespoons icing sugar
a few drops each of red,

yellow, orange, green,
brown and purple food
colouring
fruit flavourings (optional)
a few cloves
Makes 450g/1lb, enough for
about 45 little fruits

Beat the egg white lightly with a fork. Put the sugar and water in a heavy saucepan, and set it over a moderate heat. Cook, stirring often, till the sugar has dissolved. When the syrup is clear, boil it to 116°C/240°F, the soft ball stage (see page 10). Take the pan off the heat, dip its base in cold water to prevent further cooking, and stir the syrup till it begins to look cloudy. Stir in the almonds and then the egg white. Put the pan over a gentle heat and cook, stirring, for a minute or two, till the paste thickens. Take the pan off the heat and stir in the lemon juice. Sieve the icing sugar on to a work surface and turn the marzipan out on to it. Leave the marzipan till it feels cool and firm, then knead it lightly for about 5 minutes, till it is smooth.

To make marzipan fruits, divide the marzipan into portions and knead a few drops of colouring into each portion, along with the appropriate flavouring if you like. If you do not want to use the marzipan immediately, wrap each portion in

clingfilm and put them all in a plastic bag. Stored in the fridge, the marzipan will keep in good condition for at least 2 months.

*Strawberries*   For each berry, take a small piece of red marzipan. Roll it into a ball, then form it into a strawberry shape, one end pointed and the other rounded with a slight indentation. Roll the strawberry in granulated sugar to represent the seeds, and make a hull from green marzipan.
*Lemons*   Roll yellow marzipan into a ball, then into a slightly elongated shape, with each end slightly pointed. To give the surface a dimpled texture, like lemon skin, gently roll the ball over a fine grater. Use the tip of a clove for a calyx at one end, and the stem of a clove for the stem at the other.
*Bananas*   Roll a piece of yellow marzipan into a sausage shape and flatten the ends slightly. Bend it into a crescent. Using a fine paintbrush and brown food colouring or gravy browning, paint on brown stripes and markings.
*Oranges*   Roll orange marzipan into a ball. Dimple it and give it a calyx and stem in the same way as for the lemons.
*Pears*   Roll plain marzipan into a ball, them mould it into a pear shape, with one end rounded and the other pointed. Use a clove for the calyx and stem, and paint the pear with green and brown food colouring.
*Grapes*   Roll tiny balls of green or purple marzipan and press them together to form a bunch of grapes. Use a clove for the stem.

17

*450g/1lb marzipan (see page 16)*
*a few drops each of cochineal and green food colouring*
*flavourings (optional)*
*plain chocolate, broken in pieces*

*preserved stem ginger*
*walnut halves*
*dates*
*caster sugar (optional)*

Makes about 700g/1½lb

Divide the marzipan into 3 portions. Colour one pink, one green and leave the third plain. If you like, add flavourings as well – a few drops of vanilla essence, for instance, a little rosewater, or a spoonful of a liqueur such as cointreau.

*Ginger Marzipan*   Melt plain chocolate in a bowl set over a pan of hot water, off the heat. Drain some pieces of preserved stem ginger and cut them into triangles. Roll pieces of plain marzipan into balls, then flatten them slightly into rounds. Dip the base of each round in the melted chocolate and top it with a triangle of ginger.

*Walnut Sandwiches*   Roll pieces of green marzipan into balls. Press each ball between two walnut halves.

*Marzipan Rounds*   Roll pieces of pink marzipan into balls and flatten them slightly. Press a tiny ball of plain marzipan into the top of each round.

*Stuffed Dates*   Make a slit in the top of each date and take out the stone. Mould a piece of plain marzipan into an oval and push it into the space left by the stone. Press the date round the filling to re-create the original shape. If you like, roll the dates in caster sugar to give them a frosted finish.

# · PEPPERMINT CREAMS ·

1 egg white
225–275g/8–10oz icing sugar,
    sieved
a few drops of peppermint
    essence

a few drops of green food
    colouring

Makes about 225g/8oz

Line a wire rack with greaseproof paper. Beat the egg white with a fork till it is foamy. Put 225g/8oz of the icing sugar into a bowl and stir in the egg white. You need a paste that is firm enough to roll out, so add more icing sugar if necessary. Stir in the peppermint essence a drop at a time, taking care that you don't add too much. Add the food colouring and knead the mixture for a few minutes, till it is smooth and pliable.

Dust a work surface and a rolling pin with sieved icing sugar and roll out the mixture to a thickness of about 5mm/¼inch. Use small biscuit or *petits fours* cutters to cut out shapes. Place the sweets in a single layer on the wire rack, put more greaseproof paper on top of them, and leave them to dry in a warm, airy place for 24 hours. If you want to store them, leave them for another day, to dry further, then pack them in an airtight container. They will keep for about 2 weeks.

# · SUGAR MICE ·

1 egg white
450g/1lb icing sugar, sieved
2 tablespoons golden syrup
a few drops of cochineal
20 shiny pink or silver
    dragees (the kind used for
    decorating cakes)

10 lengths of narrow white or
    pink ribbon

Makes 10 mice

Line a wire rack with greaseproof paper. Whisk the egg white lightly with a fork. Put half the icing sugar into a bowl, add the egg white and the golden syrup, and beat the mixture till it is smooth. Beat in the rest of the sugar. For pink mice, add a few drops of cochineal. Knead the paste for a few minutes, till it is pliable. Divide it into 10 pieces.

To shape a mouse, take one piece, nip off a tiny bit and leave it to one side, then roll the rest into a ball. Flatten the ball slightly and draw it out into a mouse shape, with one end pointed for the nose. Press in 2 shiny pink or silver dragees for the eyes. Shape the little bit of paste to make the ears. Make small holes for the ears in the head end of the mouse, and push them in. Make a hole at the other end and push in a length of ribbon for the tail. Shape the rest of the mice in the same way. Put the mice on the wire rack, cover them with greaseproof paper and leave them to dry in a warm, airy place for 2 days. If you want to store the mice, wrap them in cellophane and keep them in an airtight container. They will keep for several months.

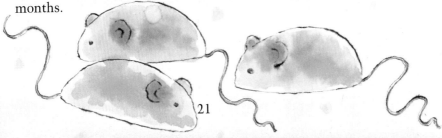

# · CREAM TOFFEES ·

*225g/8oz granulated sugar*
*225ml/8fl oz double cream*
*25g/1oz salted butter*

*3 tablespoons golden syrup*
*1 tablespoon liquid glucose*
Makes about 350g/12oz

Line a 15–18cm/6–7inch square tin with buttered greaseproof paper. Put the sugar, cream, butter, golden syrup and glucose in a heavy saucepan and set it over a moderate heat. Cook, stirring frequently and occasionally wiping down crystals from the sides of the pan with a wet pastry brush, till all the sugar has melted. Boil the mixture, stirring it fairly often to prevent it sticking, to 121°C/250°F, the firm ball stage. Take the pan from the heat and dip its base in cold water for a few seconds to halt the cooking. Drop a teaspoon of the mixture into a bowl of cold water to test that it has reached the firm ball stage (see page 10). If it is still too soft, return the pan to the heat, cook a little longer, then test again. When the consistency is right, pour the toffee quickly into the prepared tin.

Leave the toffee for a couple of hours to set, then turn it out of the tin and use an oiled knife to cut it into squares or oblongs. Wrap the toffees individually in pieces of waxed paper or cellophane, or sweet wrappers from specialist kitchen shops. Stored in a cool place, they will keep for about 2 weeks.

*Vanilla or Mint Toffees*   Stir in about 1 teaspoon of vanilla essence or a few drops of peppermint essence just before the end of cooking.

*Honey Toffees*   Replace the golden syrup and liquid glucose with 4 tablespoons of clear honey.

*Treacle Toffees*   Combine 450g/1lb of Demerara sugar, 100g/4oz of butter and 300ml/½pint of black treacle in a pan and heat gently till the sugar has dissolved. Boil, without stirring, to 138°C/280°F, the soft crack stage. Pour into a greased and lined tin and leave to set.

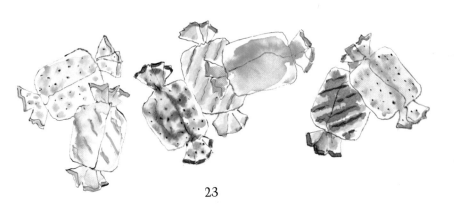

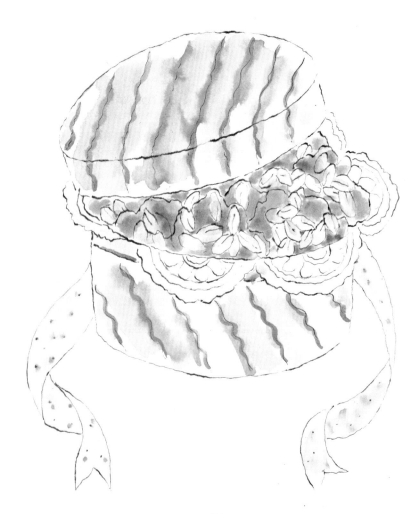

# · PEANUT BRITTLE ·

*275g/10oz raw, unsalted*
 *peanuts*
*450g/1lb granulated sugar*
*150ml/¼pint water*

Makes about 600g/1¼lb

Oil a marble slab or a baking sheet. Roast the peanuts in a
preheated moderate oven (170°C/325°F/gas mark 3) for about 10
minutes. Tip them out on to a clean towel, fold the towel over
them and rub to remove their skins. Keep them warm. Put the
sugar and water in a heavy saucepan. Cook over a moderate
heat, stirring often and occasionally wiping down sugar crystals
from the sides of the pan with a wet pastry brush, till all the
sugar has dissolved. Then, without stirring, boil till the
temperature reaches 160°C/320°F and the syrup is a pale honey-
gold colour, the light caramel stage (see page 11). Quickly but
gently, stir in the warmed nuts. Pour the mixture on to the
oiled surface in as thin a layer as possible. Spread it out further
with an oiled palette knife. Put some oil on your hands and, as
soon as the brittle is cool enough to handle (but make sure it *is*
cool enough — don't burn your hands), stretch and pull the
edges till the brittle is as thin as you can make it. Leave it till
it is cool and hard, then break it in pieces. To store the brittle,
pack it in an airtight container between sheets of waxed paper.

You can use whatever nuts you like to make a brittle. Small
nuts, such as hazelnuts, cashews and almonds, can be left
whole, while larger nuts, such as Brazil nuts or walnuts, should
be chopped into pieces.

# · CHOCOLATE FUDGE ·

*350g/12oz granulated sugar*
*50g/2oz butter, cut in little*
  *pieces*
*225ml/8fl oz milk*

*100g/4oz plain chocolate,*
  *grated*

Makes about 450g/1lb

Butter a 10–13cm/4–5inch square tin. Put the sugar, butter and milk in a heavy saucepan and stir over a moderate heat till the butter has melted and the sugar has dissolved. Boil the syrup, stirring fairly often to prevent it sticking, to 116°C/240°F, the soft ball stage (see page 10). Take the pan from the heat, dip its base in cold water to prevent further cooking, and immediately beat in the grated chocolate. Go on beating for several minutes, till the mixture thickens. Tip it into a buttered tin. Leave the fudge in a cool place to set for an hour or so, then, using an oiled knife, cut it into squares. Stored in an airtight tin between sheets of waxed paper, fudge will keep for several weeks.

# · DIVINITY ·

50g/2oz walnuts, roughly
    chopped
225g/8oz granulated sugar
2 tablespoons liquid glucose
75ml/3fl oz water

1 egg white
50g/2oz glacé cherries
½ teaspoon vanilla essence

Makes about 350g/12oz

[For this recipe, you also need an electric whisk or a helpful friend.]

Line a tray with baking parchment or waxed paper. Warm the chopped walnuts in a moderate oven (180°C/350°F/gas mark 4) for 5 minutes and keep them warm till they are needed. Put the egg white in a large bowl and whip it till it is stiff. Put the sugar, glucose and water in a heavy saucepan and cook over a moderate heat, stirring often, till all the sugar has dissolved. Boil the syrup, without stirring, to 130°C/266°F, the hard ball stage (see page 10). Take the pan from the heat and, whisking all the time, pour the syrup, in a thin, steady stream, into the egg white (either use an electric whisk or get a friend to pour as you whisk). When all the syrup has been incorporated, continue to whisk till the mixture is stiff. Fold in the cherries, the warmed nuts and the vanilla essence. Drop teaspoons of the divinity on the prepared tray and leave them to dry. Divinity is best eaten immediately, while it is fresh.

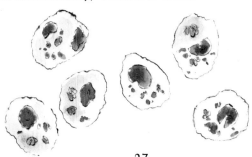

# · ALMOND NOUGAT ·

225g/8oz almonds                   225g/8oz granulated sugar
rice paper                         125ml/4fl oz water
125ml/4fl oz clear honey           1 teaspoon vanilla essence
1 egg white                        Makes about 450g/1lb

[You need an electric hand whisk or a friend for this recipe, too.]

Put the almonds in a pan of boiling water and parboil them for about 1 minute. Drain the nuts and, when they are just cool enough to handle, slip them from their skins. Chop them roughly, and keep them warm in a low oven (140°C/275°F/gas mark 1) till they are needed.

Line a baking sheet with rice paper. Pour the honey into a jug and put the jug in a bowl of hot water to warm. Put the egg white in a large bowl and beat it till it is stiff. Put a saucepan of water on to simmer.

Place the sugar and water in a heavy saucepan and set it over a moderate heat. Cook, stirring often, and occasionally wiping the sugar crystals from the sides of the pan with a wet pastry brush, till the sugar has dissolved. Boil the syrup to 138°C/280°F, the soft crack stage (see page 10). Pour in the warmed honey, and continue to cook till the temperature reaches 143°C/290°F. Take the pan from the heat and dip its base in cold water to stop the syrup cooking.

This is where you need the second pair of hands. Whisking all the time, pour the syrup in a thin stream into the beaten egg white. When all the syrup has been incorporated, put the bowl over the pan of simmering water. Whisk the mixture hard till it thickens and becomes stiff. Fold in the warmed almonds and the vanilla essence, then scoop out the nougat on to the prepared baking sheet. Use a metal spoon or palette knife dipped in hot water to spread it out evenly to a depth of

1–2cm/$\frac{1}{2}$–$\frac{3}{4}$inch. Put more rice paper on top, a board on top of the paper and some heavy weights on the board. Leave the nougat to set overnight. The next day, remove the weights and the board and, using a large, heavy knife, trim the edges of the nougat and cut it into bars or squares.

To store nougat, wrap the sweets in cellophane or greaseproof paper and put them in an airtight container. They will keep well for several weeks.

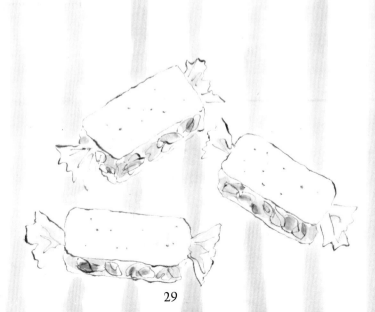

# · ORANGE LOLLIPOPS ·

*150ml/¼pint orange juice*
*450g/1lb granulated sugar*
*1 tablespoon liquid glucose*

Makes about 30 lollipops

Oil a marble slab or a baking sheet. Put the orange juice, sugar and glucose in a heavy saucepan and set it over a moderate heat. Cook, stirring often and occasionally wiping down sugar crystals from the sides of the pan with a wet pastry brush, till all the sugar has melted. Boil the syrup to 143°C/290°F, the soft crack stage (see page 10). Take the pan off the heat and dip its base in cold water to stop further cooking.

Use a dessert spoon to drop the syrup on to the oiled surface, so that it spills out into rounds about 5cm/2inches across. Push a lollipop stick into each round, then spoon a little more syrup over each stick to hold it firmly in place. When the lollipops have set hard, use a palette knife to lift them carefully from the oiled surface. Wrap them in pieces of cellophane or greaseproof paper, and store them in an airtight container.

Use other fruit juices, such as lemon, raspberry, lime or blackcurrant, to make differently flavoured and coloured lollipops.

*\* Note* If the syrup begins to set in the saucepan while you are forming the lollipops, put it back over a gentle heat to melt it again.

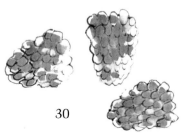

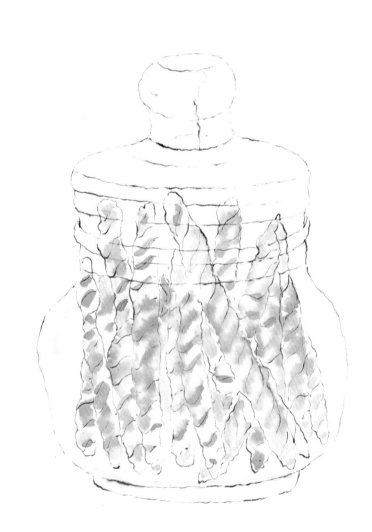

# · BARLEY SUGAR ·

*450g/1lb granulated sugar*
*150ml/¼pint water*
*juice of ½ lemon, strained*
*¼ teaspoon cream of tartar*

Makes about 25 15cm/6inch
sticks

Oil a large baking sheet. Line a tray with baking parchment or waxed paper. Put the sugar and water in a heavy saucepan and cook over a moderate heat, stirring often and occasionally wiping down the sugar crystals from the sides of the pan with a wet pastry brush, till the sugar has dissolved and the syrup is clear. Stir in the lemon juice and the cream of tartar, then bring the syrup to the boil and boil it to 154°C/310°F, the hard crack stage (see page 10). Dip the bottom of the pan briefly in cold water to stop the mixture cooking.

Pour out the syrup on the oiled baking sheet. Leave it for about 5 minutes, till it is cool enough to handle, then use oiled scissors to cut it into narrow strips. As you cut each strip, curl it by twisting the ends in opposite directions. Leave the strips on the prepared tray to set hard. To store the barley sugar sticks, wrap each one in a piece of cellophane and keep them in an airtight container.

\* *Note*   If any of the sheet of syrup sets before it can be cut and shaped, put it in a warm oven (170°C/325°F/gas mark 3) for a few minutes to soften it again.

Dipping sweets in chocolate is great fun. And, although it takes skill and experience to achieve smooth, glossy perfection, it is surprisingly easy to produce chocolates that look appealing, and taste wonderful.

Fruits, nuts and almost any sweet centre can be coated in chocolate. Fruits such as grapes, cherries, strawberries and tangerine segments; nuts, especially Brazil nuts and almonds; peppermint creams (page 20), cream toffees (page 22), fudge (page 26), nougat (page 28), truffles (page 42) — all of these are delectable with a chocolate coating. Marzipan makes a useful as well as a delicious centre, because it can be moulded or cut into any shape you like, or combined with other fillings (pages 16, 18, 38). Chocolate will slip off a wet or sticky surface, though, so make sure that whatever centres you use are quite dry. Sweets should be made a day in advance.

Line a tray with baking parchment or waxed paper. Have the centres ready. Break up the chocolate and put it in a wide bowl. Use at least 225g/8oz of chocolate, much more if you can — it is far easier to dip centres in a large pool of chocolate than in a small amount (any chocolate left over can be stored, once it has hardened, in an airtight container for future use). Bring a saucepan of water to the boil, take it off the heat and put the bowl of chocolate on top. Keeping moisture out of the chocolate is important — even a little steam condensing on it can stiffen it so that it is unusable. So always melt chocolate in a wide bowl set over a smaller saucepan.

Stir the chocolate when it has melted. Check the temperature with a sugar thermometer. The ideal temperature for dipping is 32°–43°C/90°–110°F; the chocolate must certainly not become any warmer than 49°C/120°F, or the taste and texture will be spoiled.

Partly coating a centre with chocolate is simple enough for

small children to do — and children love doing it! If you are part-dipping a fruit with a stalk, such as a grape, a cherry or a strawberry, hold it by the stalk; otherwise, hold the centre to be dipped by one end. Dip it into the chocolate, hold it over the bowl for a few seconds to let surplus chocolate drip off, then put it on the prepared tray to set.

If you want your sweets to be totally covered, drop one centre at a time into the chocolate. Turn it with a fork to make sure it is all covered with chocolate, then lift it out with the fork, balancing it on the end of the prongs. Wipe the bottom of the fork on the edge of the bowl to remove drips. Slip the chocolate off the fork on to the prepared tray to set.

If you like, leave each chocolate for about a minute, to dry just a little, then decorate it using the fork. To make straight ridges, lay the prongs of the fork across the chocolate and lift the fork slightly. Pull the fork towards you to remove it from the chocolate. To make ridges with tails in the middle, lay the prongs across the chocolate, lift the fork a bit, then move it very slightly sideways as you lift it off. Or you can leave the chocolates to dry completely, then, using a piping bag fitted

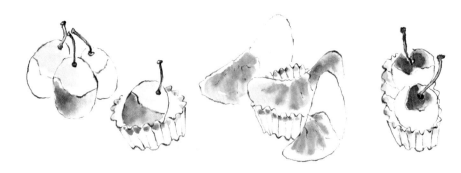

with a very fine nozzle, pipe a design in the same or a contrasting chocolate.

The length of time dipped chocolates will keep varies according to the centres you coat. Most keep well in a cool place for at least a few days but, of course, dipped fruits must be eaten while they are very fresh — this is not usually a problem!

# · CHOCOLATE CHERRIES ·

*225g/8oz marzipan (see page 16)*
*30 glacé or drained maraschino cherries*
*225g/8oz dark chocolate, broken in pieces*

*50g/2oz light chocolate, broken in pieces (optional)*

Makes 30 chocolate cherries

Line a tray with baking parchment or waxed paper. Divide the marzipan into 30 pieces and mould each piece round a cherry. Put the dark chocolate in a wide bowl. Bring a saucepan of water to the boil, take it off the heat and set the bowl of chocolate on top. When the chocolate has melted, dip the cherries into it, one by one (see page 36). As you lift each cherry out, put it on the tray to dry. If you like, when the cherries are dry, melt the light chocolate, use it to fill a piping bag fitted with a fine nozzle and pipe a design on each chocolate cherry. Store the chocolate cherries in a cool place.

*\* Note* Use dark dipping chocolate or plain eating chocolate to coat the cherries. It is best to use light dipping chocolate for the decoration — melted milk chocolate is really too thick for delicate piping.

*100g/4oz hazelnuts*
*250g/9oz plain chocolate,*
  *broken in pieces*
*100g/4oz sultanas or raisins*
*25g/1oz mixed peel*

Makes 475g/1lb 2oz, enough
for about 50 sweets

Preheat the oven to 170°C/325°F/gas mark 3. Spread the
hazelnuts on a baking tray and toast them in the oven for
about 10 minutes. Melt 200g/7oz of the chocolate in a large
bowl set over a pan of hot water. Rub the nuts in a clean cloth
to remove most of their skins. You can rub off some of the
more stubborn pieces of skin between your finger and thumb,
but don't worry if some bits still cling: they won't show and
the taste of the sweets won't be spoiled. Line a tray with
baking parchment or waxed paper.

Tip the hazelnuts, the sultanas and the mixed peel into the
melted chocolate and stir well to make sure everything is
thoroughly combined and well coated with the chocolate. Drop
teaspoons of the mixture on to the prepared tray. Leave the
sweets to set for an hour or so, then melt the remaining 50g/
2oz of chocolate and trickle a little from a teaspoon over each
nut cluster; or dip the nut clusters in melted chocolate (see
page 36). Store them in a cool place.

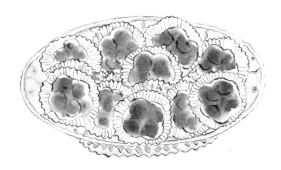

# · EASTER EGGS ·

To make Easter eggs you need only good hard chocolate —
dipping chocolate or plain eating chocolate (see pages 8–9) —
and plastic or metal moulds. Moulds are easily available,
especially at Easter time, from kitchen shops and the kitchen
departments of large stores. Transparent plastic moulds are the
easiest to use: chocolate shrinks as it sets, and with a
transparent mould it is possible to see when the chocolate has
shrunk away from the sides.

Wash the moulds in warm water, dry them carefully and
then polish their inner surfaces with a soft cloth or a ball of
cotton wool. If the moulds are well polished the chocolate will
come away easily, and the Easter eggs will have a good shine.
Line a tray with non-stick baking parchment or waxed paper.

Put the chocolate in a bowl. Bring a saucepan of water to the
boil, take it from the heat and set the bowl over it. Stir the
chocolate when it has melted.

To coat a mould, take it in your hand and spoon in enough
melted chocolate to cover its surface. Tilt the mould so that
the surface is completely coated, then tip any surplus chocolate
back into the bowl. Turn the mould upside down on the
prepared tray and put it in a cool place, for half an hour or so,
till the chocolate is firm. Cover the first layer with a second
layer, applied in the same way. If you are making a large egg,
you may need a third coat. After you have applied the final
coat, leave the mould for several hours, till the chocolate has
set quite hard and shrunk away from the sides. Run your
thumbnail between the top edge of the chocolate and the
mould, to free the chocolate shell. Slip it from its mould.

To join the two halves of the egg, brush the edge of one half
with melted chocolate and press the two halves gently
together. When the chocolate has set you can tie a ribbon
round the egg to cover the join or, using a piping bag fitted
with a star nozzle, pipe a ribbon of chocolate round it.

*225g/8oz plain chocolate,*
*broken in pieces*
*about 1 teaspoon brandy*
*75ml/3fl oz double cream*
*4 tablespoons cocoa powder*

*grated chocolate, icing sugar*
*or grated nuts, for coating*
*(optional)*

Makes about 275g/10oz

Put the chocolate into a bowl. Bring a saucepan of water to the boil, take it off the heat and set the bowl over it. Stir the chocolate when it has melted. Add the brandy to the cream and heat the mixture till it is lukewarm. Stir the flavoured cream into the melted chocolate. Leave the chocolate paste for a few minutes to cool and thicken slightly, then whisk it till it is fluffy and has lightened in colour. Put it in the fridge for about 10 minutes, till it is firm enough to handle.

Sieve the cocoa powder on to a tray, and drop teaspoons of the chocolate paste on to the cocoa. Dip your fingertips in the cocoa, then pick up each bit of chocolate paste, quickly shape it into a ball, put it back on the tray and roll it in the cocoa to cover it completely. If you like, you can give the truffles an outer coating of grated chocolate, icing sugar or grated nuts. Or you can dip them in chocolate (see page 36). Cream truffles will keep for a few days in a covered container in the fridge.

*Rum or Liqueur Cream Truffles*   Instead of the brandy, you can use a teaspoon of rum or of any liqueur of your choice.

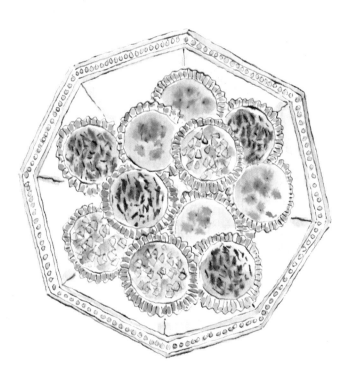

# · PIPED VANILLA TRUFFLES ·

*225g/8oz plain chocolate*
*100g/4oz unsalted butter, at*
*  room temperature*
*50g/2oz icing sugar, sieved*

*about 1 teaspoon vanilla*
*  essence*

Makes about 350g/12oz

Put the chocolate into a bowl. Bring a saucepan of water to the boil, take it from the heat and set the bowl on top. Beat the butter till it is creamy. Beat in the sugar and the vanilla essence. When the chocolate has melted, stir it and leave it for a few minutes to cool slightly, then stir it into the butter and sugar mixture. Spoon the chocolate paste into a piping bag fitted with a star nozzle and pipe the paste into foil sweet cases or doubled-up paper cases. Leave the truffles to set in the fridge, or in a cool place. Stored in the fridge, in a covered container, they will keep for about 2 weeks.

*Coffee Truffles*   Replace the vanilla essence with a teaspoon of instant coffee dissolved in a teaspoon of hot water.

*Hazelnut Truffles*   Half fill the sweet cases with the vanilla or coffee truffle mixture, pop a lightly toasted hazelnut on top and pipe in the rest of the mixture.

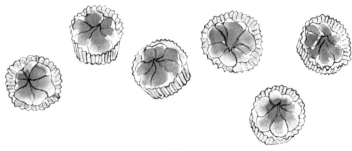

*A delightful first book for very young children which shows familiar objects found in and around the home. The baby character shown on many of the pages reflects how the object is used.*

*Encourage your child to talk about the object and ask simple questions such as – What colour is this? Where do we keep this? When do we see this?*

*The most important thing is to make looking at the book fun for both of you!*

*Acknowledgment*
The publishers would like to thank Maureen Hallahan for the hand lettering used in this book.

British Library Cataloguing in Publication Data

Ross, Sarah
    Baby's first book
    I. Title
    741    NC242.R6/
    ISBN 0-7214-1082-0

First edition

Published by Ladybird Books Ltd  Loughborough  Leicestershire  UK
Ladybird Books Inc  Lewiston  Maine 04240  USA

Printed in England

# Baby's first book

*illustrated by* SARAH ROSS

Ladybird Books

doll

teddy bear

book

blocks

car

bus

ball

# balloons

cup

# bowl and
# spoon

apple

# banana

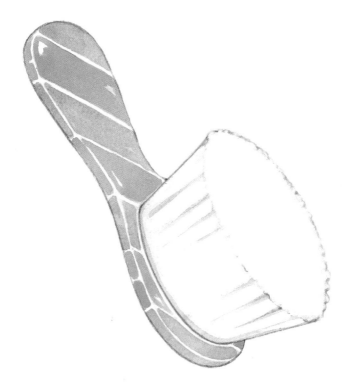

brush

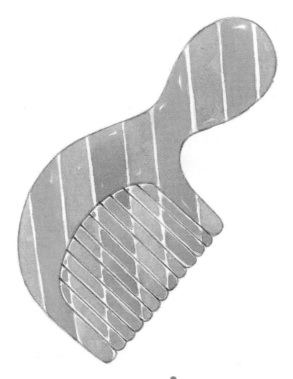

comb

soap

# sponge

kitten

# puppy

clock

telephone

hat

mittens

tree

# flowers